Performance Assessment in Orchestra

by Wendy Barden

To my mom, with love.

ISBN-10: 0-8497-2611-5
ISBN-13: 978-0-8497-2611-8

2

Table of Contents

Assessment for Learning

Students join orchestra to learn to play an instrument. Students expect to play that instrument well as a result of their enrollment and continued participation in the program. Their parents, the school board, and the community-at-large have the same expectation.

How is achievement — the orchestra's performance — usually assessed? By how well the ensemble performs at the concert, of course! Student musicians and audience members generally approach a performance as if it is a culminating event, a demonstration of the learning that has taken place since the last concert. The goal is always for the ensemble to perform at the highest possible level.

But there is another side to assessment. It is also the multi-faceted and ongoing process of gathering information prior to a culminating event — information that helps students and teachers work together to maximize learning. The recurring goal of effective directors is for the orchestra to be able to play each piece better from one rehearsal to the next while there's still time to improve before a public performance. These directors start every rehearsal with a well-developed plan and are alert to listen, ready to give specific feedback with strategies to improve the performance, willing to rehearse sections again and again before moving to another piece in the folder, and careful to make notes of skills or concepts to address at the next rehearsal.

Educational leaders outside of music education, including Paul Black, Rick Stiggins, and Grant Wiggins refer to the multi-faceted and ongoing process of assessment that promotes student achievement as *assessment for learning*. Four principles behind assessment for learning can help you lead your orchestra to perform at its highest level:

1. **Assessment must drive instruction.** Plans for Tuesday's rehearsal must come out of the ensemble's rehearsal on Monday. The most effective directors know that "winging it" doesn't propel the ensemble very far. The most effective directors are also willing to re-teach a concept or skill that isn't yet mastered by all students, and continue to ask themselves, "How can I help students learn more?" and "How can I help the performance improve?"

2. **Performance goals must be dissected.** Smaller, specific skills or concepts must be learned separately before they can be successfully combined to meet standards and produce a refined performance. Students will be able to play the A Major scale in running eighth notes if they know the finger patterns and can play the scale slowly before gradually increasing the tempo.

3. Feedback must be specific and frequent. Learning is much more efficient when students don't have to guess what is "right" or "wrong" with their performance. It's not easy to play under a director who says, "No, that's not right. Go back to letter C and play it again." It's a big assumption to believe everyone in the ensemble knows why they are going back to letter C, let alone how to improve their performance.

4. Students and teachers must be partners in learning. There was a time when teachers were considered the experts, the holders of the wisdom. No more. When students are actively involved in setting goals and monitoring their own progress, achievement increases. The students' ability to self-assess is also critical to effective practicing outside of rehearsal.

A high level of performance is likely when assessment drives instruction, skills and concepts are practiced separately and then combined, feedback is timely and specific, and students are actively involved in their learning. Success in an ensemble is motivating! It begets the confidence, desire, and willingness to work to achieve more, and there *is* more to achieve.

Take assessment for learning one step further. The key to maximizing the performance of an ensemble is to help *each student* maximize his or her personal achievement.

Remember the last time you listened to the orchestra play a particular section of a piece and thought, "This piece sounds pretty good today." But when you went back to letter D and had the low strings play you thought, "We need more work on this section." Then you asked each student in the bass section to play and thought, "Yikes! We won't be ready by next month's concert." When the performance of each individual musician improves, the performance of the full ensemble will improve.

The intention of this book is to share practical, research-based strategies for maximizing student performance in orchestra using assessment — assessment for learning. Critical to these strategies is providing feedback to individual students in a way that each student receives the feedback, knows what to do to improve, and has the opportunity to do so before he or she performs in a concert or has a score written in ink in the grade book.

It can be tricky to give individual students feedback when the ensemble is large or there is minimal rehearsal time, but it's not impossible.

◆ *When can you listen to individual students play?* A discussion of assessment management begins on page 8. ➤➤

◆ *What can you tell students to help their performance improve?* Sample comments for specific feedback begin on page 14. ➤➤

◀❙▶ *How can you efficiently and effectively provide feedback to individual students?* A variety of feedback forms begins on page 18. ➤➡

Instead of thinking "yes, but…" consider "yes, and…." When assessment is used effectively, the orchestra's next performance will be at the highest possible level!

The Teaching and Learning Cycle

The most effective orchestra directors structure their teaching on assessment for learning principles. Practically speaking, this means they pace instruction to move ahead when there is evidence of learning, not because a skill or concept has been taught. This is the same process of teaching and learning that takes place when you work with students individually, or when students study with a private studio teacher. It is likely, however, that most students in your program have you as their only teacher. How then can you structure your large group rehearsals and sectionals to support individual student achievement?

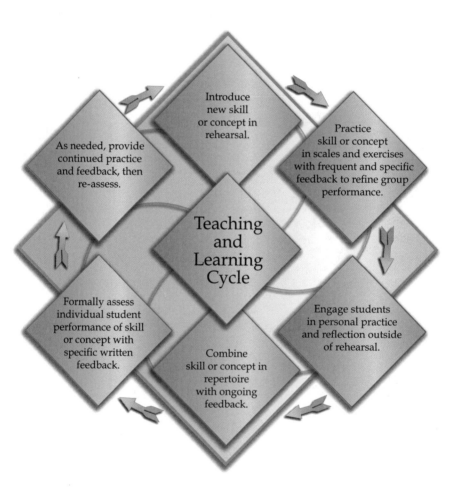

Begin your rehearsal planning by looking at the scope and sequence of the ensemble curriculum. Dissect goals into smaller, specific *skills and concepts* that, built one upon the next, join together to meet state or district standards in performance ensembles. Introduce and focus on just one or two skills or concepts at a time. During the warm-up, practice the skills and concepts in scales and exercises, and then apply the same skills and concepts in concert repertoire. Provide *specific and frequent feedback* to the full group, sections, stand partners, and individual students to help them refine their performance. Keep asking yourself, "How can I help students play this better the next time?"

When it is time to *formally assess* the learning of individual students, stay focused. Tell students exactly which few skills or concepts you will be assessing. You can't listen and watch for "everything" because the list is extensive:

Key signature	Tone
Pitches	Dynamics
Fingerings	Phrasing
Intonation	Vibrato
Rhythms	Posture
Bowing style	Left hand position
Bow usage	Bow hold
Technique	

(prioritize?)

Assign an exercise or excerpt that is long enough for the student to be able to demonstrate the identified skills or concepts consistently, and that makes musical sense. Usually eight to sixteen measures is sufficient in $\frac{3}{4}$ or $\frac{4}{4}$ time, and sixteen to thirty-two measures in $\frac{2}{2}$ or a fast $\frac{6}{8}$ time. Students should play from the beginning of the music and stop at the end of the theme, section, or exercise. This short, focused assignment requires about thirty seconds per student.

To facilitate *written feedback* on the assessment, duplicate or modify one of the various feedback forms in this book (pages 40-48). ➤➤ Give or show students a copy of the feedback form a few days prior to the assessment and discuss it so they know what to expect. The form also holds you accountable to listen to each student consistently. Then, as each student plays for the assessment, jot notes on the form to capture the essence of the performance. After rehearsal, go back and fill in the missing words or phrases so the comments will make more sense. Feedback must be specific so each student knows what to do to play better the next time, and must be conveyed in a manner and tone that students will accept. Make note of the students' achievement in your record book and return the written feedback the next day of class. As needed, have students use the feedback, continue to practice, and *replay the assessment* for you in one week. What is the incentive? The opportunity to replace the first score with the one earned in the replay.

Manage the assessment process. If you see your students in lessons or sectionals on a regular basis, you may easily conduct individual playing assessments during that time. The only new step for you might be focusing on basic skills and concepts, improving the quality of your feedback, or building in the opportunity for students to work with the feedback and replay the assessment at a later date.

Frequent individual playing assessments within the orchestra rehearsal require strategic and creative testing management. How much time should be devoted to hearing individual students play the assessments, and what do the other students do while they wait? Here are four ideas for managing individual performance assessments during large ensemble rehearsals, each with advantages and considerations:

1. Perform During Rehearsal. Students perform individually from their place in the ensemble.

Advantages	Additional Considerations
◆ This allows accurate observation of elements such as tone quality, intonation, bowing, hand position, and posture. ◆ All students stay under the teacher's supervision. ◆ Minimal teacher time is needed outside rehearsal to listen to students and to write feedback.	◆ Keep the exercise or excerpt brief and focused on the objective. ◆ Provide other students with a written activity related to the repertoire such as theory, terms and symbols, or composition. As a last resort make the day a "study hall." ◆ For a student who is reluctant to play in front of peers, offer to listen to his or her exercise outside of class *prior* to the testing day.

2. Record During Class Time. Students leave class individually to go to a practice room and record their performance.

Advantages	Additional Considerations
◈ There is little interruption to the full ensemble rehearsal. ◈ Recorders can be set up in multiple practice rooms. ◈ Video recording will allow the observation of physical aspects of playing including hand position, posture, and bowing.	◈ Model how to use the equipment to ensure audible performances and so no recordings are inadvertently erased or lost. ◈ Have a student aide or parent volunteer stationed in the recording area to run the equipment. ◈ The quality of audio recording equipment might limit assessment elements to just pitch and rhythm. ◈ When will you listen to the tapes and provide *written feedback* to students?

3. Record Outside of Class Time. Students turn in a recording of their individual performance made at home or outside of rehearsal.

Advantages	Additional Considerations
◈ There is no interruption to the full ensemble rehearsal. ◈ Students can record and re-record their performance until they are satisfied, encouraging self-assessment.	◈ The quality of audio equipment might limit assessment elements to just pitch and rhythm. ◈ Students without recording capabilities at home need time in school to be able to record their performance until satisfied. ◈ When will you listen to the tapes and provide *written feedback* to students?

4. Assessment Via Computer Software. Software programs record, score, and log each student's individual performances.

Advantages	Additional Considerations
◆ There is little or no interruption to the full ensemble rehearsal. ◆ Students get some immediate feedback. ◆ The audio quality may be significantly better than other technology, making it possible to assess elements such as tone. ◆ Students can record and re-record their performance until they are satisfied, encouraging self-assessment.	◆ Test the scoring feature of the software by playing several instruments to understand limitations relative to range and timbre. Computer-generated scores may not always be accurate. ◆ Students without computer access at home need time and resources provided in school to be able to record their performance until satisfied. ◆ When will you review each student's performance to provide *your own written feedback* to students?

Grades. While you may maximize the performance of your orchestra by making assessment an integral part of your teaching and learning cycle, how can individual student achievement be reflected in a grade at the end of the marking period? The principles of a credible grading framework parallel our discussion of assessment for learning:

◀▶ The score from one playing assignment has little meaning; gather information on student performance in multiple opportunities over time.

◀▶ The use of many shorter playing assessments provides teachers and students with more accurate evidence of learning than a few longer excerpts.

◀▶ Assessments are most accurate when there are no surprises, no secrets. Provide students with the feedback form prior to the assessment, while there is still time to practice.

◀▶ Ongoing opportunities must promote continued improvement.

  ◇ Encourage the replaying of an assessment to show developing proficiency.

  ◇ Allow the dropping of earlier scores as later ones show improvement.

  ◇ Eliminate the lowest in a series of scores focused on a single objective.

◀▶ In addition to performance, there are other skills and concepts in orchestra to be learned, formally assessed, and documented. How well does the student:

  ◇ Use music theory and terms and symbols?

  ◇ Compose and improvise?

  ◇ Analyze and describe music?

  ◇ Evaluate music and music performances?

  ◇ Know the cultural or historic context of the music?

  ◇ Relate music to another subject?

Structure your rehearsals on assessment for learning principles that address both the full ensemble performance and individual student learning within the orchestra. Identify basic skills and concepts to be learned, monitor student learning, provide specific feedback to help individual students know how to improve their performance, allow time to apply feedback, and document learning. As the performance of each individual student improves, so will the performance of the orchestra. Are you ready to implement these principles and enjoy the results at the next concert?

The Power of Specific Feedback

Every time a director cuts off the orchestra in the middle of a piece he or she is doing so to give feedback — feedback to help the group refine the performance and play the piece better the next time. If the feedback is specific, and communicated in a manner and tone that students will accept, its impact on the performance can be amazing!

The same effect can happen when individual students receive specific feedback on their performance. Feedback must provide specific information about what was accurate in the performance, and how it can be played better the next time. This shouldn't be a surprise! It is difficult to improve at anything in life without feedback, from writing essays to running marathons to playing an instrument.

Let's say a teacher frequently assigns scales and exercises, rehearses the assignments in class, listens to students play them individually, and posts a list of their numerical scores under pseudonyms. Are students receiving real feedback on their performance? If students score ten out of ten points on the assessment they know they met the objectives or criteria, but what goes through the mind of the student who scored seven or eight points? "What did I do wrong?" "I practiced hard for that test and could play it perfectly." "I'm not very good at this." "Why work as hard next time because I can't do it anyway?"

Number or letter scores alone provide some feedback but certainly don't help students know how to improve the next time. The key to maximizing the performance of an ensemble is to help *each student* maximize his or her personal achievement. To that end, specific feedback is powerful and essential.

Feedback on the individual performances should be written. Students need to have information to refer to as they are practicing, and oral comments tend to be forgotten or transformed over time. Written feedback should be given whether the performance is live or recorded, and whether the teacher listens to it in the orchestra room or in the comfort of the family room at home.

Feedback forms. Use a feedback form for your next assessment by duplicating one in this book or creating your own. If you use a form from the book, you might spend a few minutes to create your own master — two forms side-by-side and reduced as necessary. Duplicate and cut in half.

A few days prior to the playing assignment, distribute the feedback form or review the two to three specific skills that will be assessed. No surprises, no secrets. Be sure all students recognize characteristics of an exemplary performance.

During the assessment, while listening to each student play, write notes on the form to capture the essence of the performance. If the scale or exercise is performed during rehearsal, your notes will be somewhat cryptic due to time. After rehearsal, go back and fill in the missing words, symbols, or phrases so the comments will make more sense to the student. Feedback must be specific to help a student know how to play better the next time.

Most likely, there will be a few students who have not yet mastered the skill or concept assessed. Provide an incentive for them to use your feedback in practice. Encourage select students to replay the assessment in one week (before or after school, before or at the end of class, during study hall). Or, revisit the skill or concept in future assessments, and delete the lowest score.

Comments. Comments are sometimes confused with praise. "Nice job!" or "Good improvement!" can come off our pens very easily and might feel good to the student, but neither phrase provides concrete information about their performance. Constructive comments can also be conveyed in a manner and tone that feels supportive, especially when there is good rapport between you and your students.

Every feedback form in this book includes a section for comments. Use some of the sample comments on the following pages to spark the feedback you write. The goal is to help each student recognize what has been achieved and how to continue to improve his or her performance the next time.

Now is the time to sharpen your feedback skills in rehearsal. The ensemble will progress much more efficiently when students don't have to guess what is "right" or "wrong" with their performance—when they know exactly why they are going back to letter C, and how to play that section better the next time.

Specific feedback is also central to improving individual student performance within the orchestra. Get into the habit of writing commendations and constructive comments, rather than just number or letter scores, to provide students with information that will be helpful as they practice at home. Then, create an incentive for students to use the feedback and refine their performance by giving them the opportunity to replay the assignment.

Sample Comments for Specific Feedback

Element	Commendations	Suggestions for Improvement
Body Posture	◈ Your instrument was well supported today with tall posture. ◈ I liked to see you holding the instrument with your chin and shoulder. ◈ I noticed your cello is centered correctly on your body and is placed between your knees.	◈ Be sure to sit forward in your chair with more weight on your feet. ◈ Be sure that the instrument rests on your shoulder and not your collarbone. ◈ Keep your jaw nestled into the chin rest. ◈ Keep the bass in contact with your left hip when you play from a standing position.
Bow Hold	◈ I liked to see your right thumb stayed bent slightly throughout the song. ◈ Your fingers seem relaxed and curved over the stick.	◈ Remember that your pinky finger rests on top of the stick. ◈ Be sure to keep your wrist relaxed and flat. ◈ Your thumb should not poke through between the horsehair and the stick.
Left Hand and Arm	◈ Your left hand fingers maintained their curved shape throughout the exercise. ◈ I noticed you played the A with your fourth finger as marked. ◈ Good improvement today! Your thumb stayed under your second finger throughout the song.	◈ Keep your left elbow tucked well under the instrument to play notes on the G string. ◈ Avoid resting your wrist against the violin neck. Keep your hand, wrist, and arm straight. ◈ Remember to keep your first finger anchored as you cross strings. ◈ Be sure to press your left fingers firmly on the thick lower strings.

Sample Comments, *continued*

Element	Commendations	Suggestions for Improvement
Tone	◆ The solid, straight bow strokes you created today gave you a strong, full tone. ◆ Today your fingers pressed firmly on the strings so the notes sounded clearly.	◆ Each time you play be sure your bow is properly tightened. ◆ Be sure there is enough rosin on the bow to grab the strings. ◆ Use a slower bow speed when you play on your lowest string to help it vibrate.
Bow Speed and Bow Usage	◆ Today you did a good job of playing with the whole bow. ◆ I noticed you used the full bow to play each note of the exercise. Good improvement.	◆ Be sure to use the full length of the bow, frog to tip, for the longer note values. ◆ Concentrate on keeping your bow moving parallel to the bridge. ◆ For a louder sound, place your bow closer to the bridge.
Pitch Accuracy	◆ You played all the accidentals accurately today. ◆ I can tell you have been practicing the ledger line notes. You played them easily and confidently today.	◆ Check the key signature carefully. You played C♯s instead of C♮s. ◆ Remember F♮ is played with your 2nd finger. ◆ Be sure to think of the finger pattern for each string before you begin the scale.

Sample Comments, *continued*

Element	Commendations	Suggestions for Improvement
Intonation	◆ You played very precisely in tune today. ◆ I noticed you consistently placed your fingers on the tapes for accurate intonation.	◆ Listen as you play F♮ and adjust your finger placement so it isn't too high. ◆ Check your finger placement so that your 4th finger A on the D string matches the sound of your open A string.
Rhythmic Accuracy	◆ I can tell you were subdividing in your head. You played all the eighth notes evenly today. ◆ You played the dotted eighth and sixteenth rhythm precisely today. ◆ You played the complicated rhythm in measure 6 without hesitating.	◆ Be sure to hold the dotted half note for full value. ◆ Work on keeping the beat steady when you change from the quarter notes to sixteenth notes. ◆ Practice difficult rhythms on an open string before adding fingers. ◆ Practice difficult measures slowly before playing them at full speed.
Bowing style	◆ I noticed your accents were strong today. ◆ You kept your bow moving nicely on the slurs. ◆ You found the "sweet spot" where your bow bounces easily to play spiccato. ◆ You moved between strings with smooth and connected bow strokes.	◆ Pay more attention to the slurs so your bow changes direction exactly as written. ◆ Remember your arm must stop moving to create crisp staccato sounds.

Sample Comments, *continued*

Element	Commendations	Suggestions for Improvement
Technique	◆ Your shifting was quick and accurate. ◆ Today your fingers and bow were moving exactly together to produce clear, clean runs.	◆ Keep practicing to shift more quickly in measures 3 and 6. ◆ Practice the runs slowly, then gradually increase the tempo.
Phrasing	◆ You observed the bow lifts accurately to create the phrases. ◆ Dynamics were followed to nicely shape the melody.	◆ Carefully observe the down bow and up bow markings.
Overall Performance	◆ I thought your performance today sounded strong and confident. ◆ You set a good tempo today and maintained it throughout the piece.	◆ Notes, rhythms, and bowing are correct, but continue to practice to be able to play the exercise faster. ◆ Before playing, set your bow on the string, prepare your left hand, and think about the first notes in your music.

Assessing Basic Skills

Forms 1.1, 1.2, 1.3

Feedback forms in this section help both orchestra director and students think about the achievement of foundational skills. Use these forms when you are assessing the demonstration of basic skills or concepts. Duplicate one of the forms or use the ideas to spark the development of your own form that is specific to your orchestra.

Form 1.1: Early Skills

Assessment Goal	**Provide feedback to beginning students on the demonstration of basic skills or concepts.**
Considerations for Effective Use	◆ Introduce students to the form and an exemplary performance several days prior to assessment. ◆ Limit skills or concepts to two or three elements such as tone, bowing style, rhythm, key signature, accidentals, dynamic contrast, or vibrato. ◆ Select an exercise that is four to eight measures in length—just long enough to provide evidence that the student has a general mastery of the skills or concepts. ◆ Hold students accountable to replay the exercise—demonstrating any critical skills or concepts that are not yet satisfactory.

For a duplicable template of Form 1.1, go to page 40. ➤➡

For a customizable electronic version, go to the Kjos Multimedia Library at www.kjos.com.

Name ___ *Owen Thomas* ___   Date __ *10/7* __

Music Exercise ___ *#22* _____

Today's assessment focused on the three skills or concepts named below. The checked boxes show the skills or concepts demonstrated satisfactorily. Empty boxes show the skills or concepts needing more attention.

☑ Accurate pitches

☑ Steady pulse

☐ Bow speed

Comments:

Be sure to use the full length of your bow, frog to tip.

☑ Use my comments and keep practicing this exercise to continue to improve your performance. Be sure to talk to me if you have questions or need help. Replay this exercise:

Tues., Oct. 15 – before school
_____

☐ Assignment complete.

Sample Form 1.1: Early Skills

Form 1.2: Developing Fundamentals

Assessment Goal	Provide feedback to intermediate-advanced students on an overall performance.
Considerations for Effective Use	◆ Introduce students to the form and an exemplary performance several days prior to assessment. ◆ Tailor the focus of this assessment to meet varying needs of students within the large ensemble. ◆ Clearly discuss vocabulary on the form. ◆ Select an exercise that is sixteen to thirty-two measures in length—long enough to provide evidence of elements performed satisfactorily and one needing continued attention. ◆ Some students will benefit from replaying the exercise, depending on the skill or concept needing more practice.

For a duplicable template of Form 1.2, go to page 41. ➤➤➤

For a customizable electronic version, go to the Kjos Multimedia Library at www.kjos.com.

Name ___*Sue Tangor*___ Date ___*11/2*___

Music Exercise ___*Etude #11*___

The checked boxes show two elements of your performance that were particularly strong.

- ☐ Key signature
- ☐ Pitches
- ☐ Intonation
- ☑ Rhythm
- ☑ Pulse
- ☐ Bowing style
- ☐ Technique
- ☐ Tone
- ☐ Phrasing
- ☐ Dynamics

Comments:

You played the ♪♪ patterns accurately and with a steady pulse.

The checked box shows one element for you to think about as you continue to practice.

- ☐ Key signature
- ☐ Pitches
- ☐ Intonation
- ☐ Rhythms
- ☐ Pulse
- ☑ Bowing style
- ☐ Technique
- ☐ Tone
- ☐ Phrasing
- ☐ Dynamics

Comments:

Be sure to keep your bow moving as you change notes in the slurs.

☑ Use my comments and keep practicing this exercise. Be sure to talk to me if you have questions or need help. Replay exercise:

___*November 9 – during class*___

☐ Assignment complete.

Sample Form 1.2: Developing Fundamentals

Form 1.3: Individual Improvement Goal

Assessment Goal	Provide feedback to intermediate-advanced students on the skill chosen by each individual as needing continued attention.
Considerations for Effective Use	◆ Select an exercise that is sixteen to thirty-two measures in length. ◆ Every musician has one skill that needs more attention or one that could be more fully developed. In this assignment, the goal is for each student to identify, thoughtfully address, and improve a weakness, *not* attain a perfect final score. Students must clearly understand the intent of the assignment to risk working through a weakness rather than asking for feedback in an area of strength. ◆ Introduce and discuss the form with students as the exercise is introduced, challenging them to think critically about their individual strengths and weaknesses. Students should identify one area in their playing that needs improvement and complete sections 1 and 2. ◆ Have students complete section 3 as they practice. Collect the forms prior to the performance assessment so you can add your comments. ◆ This form supports differentiated instruction within the large ensemble.

For a duplicable template of Form 1.3, go to page 42. ➤➤

For a customizable electronic version, go to the Kjos Multimedia Library at www.kjos.com.

Name __*Kevin Andre*__ Date __*3/5*__

Music Exercise __*#47*__

1. What is one area that needs improvement in your playing?

☑ Notes ☐ Technique

☐ Intonation ☐ Tone

☐ Rhythm and pulse ☐ Dynamics

☐ Bowing style ☐ _____

2. Explain why you think this area needs improvement.

I'm not used to playing Bb and Eb so sometimes I play B and E by mistake.

3. What did you do when you practiced to improve in this area?

1. I circled all of the Bs and Es in the music to help me remember they are flatted.

2. I practiced the exercise slowly at first, then a little faster.

Teacher's Comments:

The key signature was accurate except the high Bb in measure 6. Practice measure 6 over and over until you can play it easily, then play the exercise straight through.

Sample Form 1.3: Individual Improvement Goal

Assessing Scales

Forms 2.1, 2.2

Feedback forms in this section help both orchestra director and students focus on the performance of scales. Duplicate one of the forms or use the ideas to spark the development of your own form that is specific to your orchestra.

Form 2.1: Early Scales

Assessment Goal	Provide feedback to beginning-intermediate students on the accuracy of notes in a one-octave scale.
Considerations for Effective Use	◆ Introduce students to the form and an exemplary performance of the scale several days prior to assessment. You might have students write the letter name next to each ascending and descending scale degree. ◆ This form limits your feedback to the correct sequence of pitches. ◆ As each student plays, circle any scale degree that is played as a wrong note. ◆ The first time you assess one-octave scales, encourage students to read the music. Hold students accountable to replay the scale, as needed. ◆ When students can play the scale satisfactorily, you might challenge them to play the scale from memory.

For a duplicable template of Form 2.1, go to page 43. ➤━▷

For a customizable electronic version, go to the Kjos Multimedia Library at www.kjos.com.

Name <u>*Ricky James*</u>　　　Date <u>*2/6*</u>

Scale <u>*C Major*</u>

Circled notes in the scale were played as a wrong note.

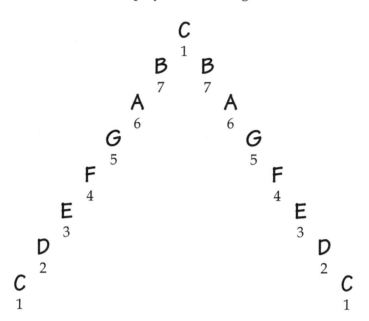

Comments:

I thought your performance today sounded strong and confident.

☐ Use my comments and keep practicing this scale to play it accurately. Be sure to talk to me if you have questions or need help. Replay this scale:

_____

☑ Scale satisfactory. Assignment complete.

Sample Form 2.1: Early Scales

Form 2.2: Scale Proficiency

Assessment Goal	Provide feedback to intermediate-advanced students as they refine their performance of scales.
Considerations for Effective Use	◆ Provide students with an exemplary performance several days prior to the assessment. Scale proficiency should go beyond pitch accuracy and include setting clear expectations for tempo and rhythm. ◆ Determine if students can use music or if the scale must be played from memory. ◆ Distribute copies of the form for students to use as they practice (and self-assess) their performance outside of class. ◆ As students play the scale, circle any area needing improvement and provide specific information to focus continued practice. ◆ Hold students accountable to replay the scale, as needed.

For a duplicable template of Form 2.2, go to page 44. ➤━▶

For a customizable electronic version, go to the Kjos Multimedia Library at www.kjos.com.

Name ___**Jill King**___ Date **4/13**

Scale ___**G Major – two octaves**___

Improvement is needed in the areas circled:

Clean Start

Correct Notes

(Intonation)

Even Tone

Steady Tempo

Expected Tempo

Comments:

In the second octave, your C♮ and G were sharp. Think carefully about the half steps between B-C and F#-G.

☑ Use my comments and keep practicing this scale. Be sure to talk to me if you have questions or need help. Replay this scale:

___**Before or after class by April 23**___

☐ Scale proficient. Assignment complete.

Sample Form 2.2: Scale Proficiency

Assessing Short Exercises

Forms 3.1, 3.2, 3.3

Feedback forms in this section help both orchestra director and students focus on achievement demonstrated through the performance of short exercises, perhaps from a method or technique book. Duplicate one of the forms or use the ideas to spark the development of your own form that is specific to your orchestra.

Form 3.1: Eight-Measure Exercise

Assessment Goal	Provide feedback to beginning-intermediate students on the performance of basic skills or concepts in an exercise.
Considerations for Effective Use	◆ Introduce students to the form and an exemplary performance of the exercise several days prior to assessment. ◆ Use exercises that are eight measures in length; each box represents one measure. ◆ Limit measure-by-measure scoring to two critical elements, such as notes and rhythm, for a possible score of eight points. Other combinations of elements might be articulation and rhythm, rudiments and rhythm, tone and notes, notes and articulation, or rhythm and dynamics. As students play, note errors in the measure they occur. ◆ Choose two more elements of lesser importance and make them worth one point each, such as posture and clean start, to give a combined total of ten possible points for the exercise. ◆ During the marking period, assess each skill or concept in several exercises. At the end of the marking period, allow students to drop their lowest score or replay up to two exercises for higher scores.

For a duplicable template of Form 3.1, go to page 45. ➤➤

For a customizable electronic version, go to the Kjos Multimedia Library at www.kjos.com.

Name ___**Eddie Scott**_____ Date _**12/9**____

Music Exercise ___**#69**_____

Notes or rhythms played incorrectly are written in each measure box:

①	②	③	④

⑤	⑥	⑦	⑧

Comments:

> *Be sure the eighth notes in measure 3 get full value.*
> *Keep your cello centered on your body and stabilized with your legs.*

Notes and Rhythm		Start		Posture		Total
7	+	**1**	+	**0**	=	**8**
(8)		(1)		(1)		(10)

Sample Form 3.1: Eight-Measure Exercise

Form 3.2: Special Focus — Rhythm

Assessment Goal	Provide extended feedback to intermediate-advanced students on the performance of a rhythm concept in multiple exercises.
Considerations for Effective Use	◆ Identify a rhythm concept on which to focus for a month or marking period, such as the four subdivisions of a quarter note shown on Form 3.2. ◆ Select four exercises, each eight to sixteen measures in length, that students will count and play to demonstrate their understanding of the rhythm. ◆ Score exercises at one point per measure (eight-measure exercise) or one point per two measures (sixteen-measure exercise). ◆ If some students have not earned full credit on an exercise, provide continued practice and feedback. The goal is for everyone to master these rhythms now and be able to use them in future repertoire. ◆ At the end of the month or marking period, allow students to repeat any of the exercises to show mastery and earn the full eight points. ◆ Revise this form to focus on other rhythm concepts in $\frac{3}{2}$ or $\frac{6}{8}$ time.

For a duplicable template of Form 3.2, go to page 46. For a duplicable template of Form 3.2, go to page 46.

For a customizable electronic version, go to the Kjos Multimedia Library at www.kjos.com.

Name _Renée Morgan_

Exercise and Rhythm	Comments	Points* (8)
# 51	Count and Clap You clapped the ♫♫ evenly. (Date: 1/4)	8
♫♫	Play Rhythm accurate! (Date: 1/8)	8
# 62	Count and Clap (Date: 1/16)	8
♫	Play You set a good tempo that you maintained throughout the exercise. (Date: 1/20)	8
# 69	Count and Clap Your clapping and counting sounded confident. (Date: 1/24)	8
♫	Play Rhythm was accurate in measures 3–8. Think about the rhythm before you start to play so measures 1–2 are accurate. (Date: 1/31)	6
# 85	Count and Clap Rhythm accurate! (Date: 2/6)	8
♫	Play I can tell you were subdividing in your head because you played the ♫ rhythm precisely. (Date: 2/12)	8

*Every exercise may be repeated on ___2/19___ to show mastery.

Sample Form 3.2: Special Focus—Rhythm

Form 3.3: Special Focus

Assessment Goal	Provide extended feedback to intermediate-advanced students on the performance of a specific skill in multiple exercises.
Considerations for Effective Use	◆ Identify one skill — or instrument-specific skill — on which to provide extended feedback. Sample Form 3.3 shows spiccato as the special focus over the period of a month.
	◆ Select four exercises, each eight to sixteen measures in length, that students will play to demonstrate their mastery of the specific skill.
	◆ Score exercises at one point per measure (eight-measure exercise) or one point per two measures (sixteen-measure exercise).
	◆ If some students have not earned full credit on an exercise, provide continued practice and feedback. The goal is for everyone to master the new skill now and be able to use it in future repertoire.
	◆ At the end of the month or marking period, allow students to repeat any of the exercises to show mastery and earn the full eight points.
	◆ This form can be used to provide extended feedback on the performance of a variety of skills or concepts such as tone, styles of bowing, vibrato, or dynamics.

For a duplicable template of Form 3.3, go to page 47. ➤▷

For a customizable electronic version, go to the Kjos Multimedia Library at www.kjos.com.

Name _____Alice Zabet_____

Special Focus_____Spiccato_____

Exercise	Comments	Points* (8)
G Major Scale	Move your bow closer to the frog to find the spot where it bounces easily. (Date: 11/2)	6
Etude #25	Your bow is bouncing more easily today. Keep practicing this etude so your left hand fingers won't slow you down. (Date: 11/9)	7
#31	Accurate bow placement and movement! You set a good tempo today that you maintained throughout the exercise. (Date: 11/16)	8
#54	Spiccato bowing sounded strong and confident today. (Date: 11/23)	8

*Every exercise may be repeated on _____11/30_____ to show mastery.

Sample Form 3.3: Special Focus

Assessing Concert Repertoire

Form 4.1

The feedback form in this section helps both orchestra director and students focus on achievement demonstrated through the performance of concert repertoire. Duplicate the form or use the ideas to create your own rubrics specific to your concert repertoire.

Form 4.1: Concert Repertoire

Assessment Goal	Provide feedback to intermediate-advanced students on the overall performance of a significant excerpt from concert repertoire.
Considerations for Effective Use	◆ Select an instrument-specific excerpt twenty-four to thirty-two measures in length. ◆ Schedule the assessment about three weeks prior to the concert, and use the information you learn to focus the work in your remaining rehearsals. ◆ Limit the rubric to five elements. ◆ Introduce students to the form several days prior to assessment. ◆ As you listen to students play, circle each element description that best represents the student's performance. Write a comment on any element of the performance in which a student scores just one point so he or she knows how to improve. ◆ Hold students scoring one point in any element accountable to replay the excerpt. ◆ After students have experienced this form of assessment using the three, two, and one point descriptions, you might identify another excerpt from concert repertoire and instruct the students in each section to identify three or four significant elements and develop descriptions for three levels of proficiency. Duplicate, distribute, and use the assessment.

For a duplicable template of Form 4.1, go to page 48. For a duplicable template of Form 4.1, go to page 48.

For a customizable electronic version, go to the Kjos Multimedia Library at www.kjos.com.

Name <u>**Tom Marlowe**</u>   Date <u>**5/1**</u>

Music Excerpt <u>**Symphony No. 2 – ⓐ to ⓑ**</u>

Instrument <u>**Viola**</u>

Element	3 points	2 points	1 point
Bowing style	Slurs, accents, and staccatos are clean and accurate.	Slurs, accents, and staccatos are mostly accurate.	Slurs, accents, and staccatos are misplayed.
Rhythm	Rhythms are accurate.	One rhythm is misplayed one or more times.	More than one rhythm is misplayed.
Dynamics	Dynamics are accurate.	Dynamics are mostly accurate.	Dynamics are misplayed.
Posture	Overall posture is excellent.	One aspect of posture is not good.	Overall posture is not good.

Total Score <u>**11**</u>

Comments:

Play the phrase marked piano even softer.

☐ Use my comments and keep practicing this excerpt to play it accurately. Be sure to talk to me if you have questions or need help. Replay this excerpt:

_____

☑ Excerpt satisfactory. Assignment complete.

Sample Form 4.1: Concert Repertoire

More Elements and Descriptions

Element	3 points	2 points	1 point
Tone	Tone is rich and full.	Tone loses its richness at times.	Tone is thin.
Notes and Accidentals	Notes and accidentals are played accurately.	At least one note or accidental is missed one or more times.	Several notes or accidentals are misplayed.
Intonation	Intonation is accurate.	Intonation is generally accurate.	Intonation is inaccurate throughout.
Technique	Coordination of fingers and bow is precise.	Coordination of fingers and bow is unclear at times.	Coordination of fingers and bow is poor throughout.
Pulse	Steady pulse is maintained.	Steady pulse is maintained with one interruption.	Pulse is not steady.
Use of the Full Bow	Full bow strokes are used throughout.	Full bow strokes are generally used.	Full bow strokes are not used throughout.
Slurs	Slurs are accurate.	Slurs are generally accurate.	Slurs are misplayed.
Accent	Accents are consistently short and powerful.	A hint of the accent is evident.	Accent strokes are not used.
Spiccato	Spiccato strokes bounce evenly and consistently.	A hint of the spiccato stroke is evident.	Spiccato strokes are not used.

Element	3 points	2 points	1 point
Musical Style	The musical style rehearsed in orchestra is conveyed.	The musical style rehearsed in orchestra is conveyed at times.	The musical style does not match the style rehearsed in orchestra.
Vibrato	Vibrato sounds controlled and adds warmth to the tone.	Vibrato is used but sounds too fast or uncontrolled.	Vibrato is not used.
Presence	The excerpt is played with confidence.	The excerpt is fumbled or restarted at some point.	The excerpt is fumbled and composure is not regained.

Bibliography

Baume, David. "Giving Feedback to Students." *First Words*. Oxford Brookes University. http://www.brookes.ac.uk/services/ocsd/ firstwords/fw21.html (accessed March 29, 2009).

Black, Paul and Dylan Wiliam. *Inside the Black Box: Raising standards through classroom assessment*. London: School of Education, King's College, 1998.

Brophy, Timothy S., ed. *Assessment in Music Education: Integrating Curriculum, Theory, and Practice*. Chicago: GIA, 2008.

Music Educators National Conference. *Spotlight on Assessment in Music Education*. Reston: MENC, 2001.

Qualifications and Curriculum Authority. "The 10 principles: Assessment for Learning." QCA. http://www.qca.org.uk/qca_4336.aspx (accessed March 23, 2009).

Stiggins, Richard J. *Student-Involved Classroom Assessment*. Upper Saddle River: Prentice-Hall, Inc., 2001.

Wiggins, Grant. *Assessing Student Performance*. San Francisco: Jossey-Bass, 1993.

Wiggins, Grant. "Grant Wiggins on Grading." http://www.grantwiggins. org/documents/GradingDAY1.pdf (accessed March 23, 2009).

Wiggins, Grant. "Assessment as Feedback." *New Horizons for Learning* X, no. 2 (2004). http://www.newhorizons.org/strategies/assess/wiggins.htm (accessed March 23, 2009).

Duplicable Forms

The forms on pages 40-48 are templates of the sample forms discussed in detail on pages 18-37, and are authorized for duplication. The templates are provided to help you easily adapt the feedback strategies to your specific classroom.

To prepare a form:

1. Photocopy the assessment form.
2. Write in the date, music exercise, elements of the assessment, and replay date, as needed.
3. To conserve the use of paper, you might take an extra minute to create a duplicable master that has two feedback forms side-by-side. Do this by photocopying the form you just adapted, discard the blank half of each page, and place the forms side-by-side on the copier glass.
4. Reduce the size as needed and duplicate the master form as needed for the number of students you have.
5. Prior to the assessment, write each student's name on a form and put the forms in the order you will hear students play. Another option is to distribute the forms, have the students write in their own names, and then collect the forms from the students.

If you prefer to make a customizable electronic version of the form:

1. Using your computer, visit the Kjos Multimedia Library at www.kjos.com.
2. Click on the Kjos Multimedia Library logo.
3. Click on "Teacher Resources."

Here, the forms are available for you to be able to create a more polished copy. These forms cannot be saved online, however, so plan to print out a master to save for future reference.

Duplication Restrictions

The duplicable resources in this book are strictly limited to the pages that include the following copyright notice:

Unauthorized duplication of any other pages in this book is prohibited. The author and publisher thank you for your strict adherence to copyright laws, and encourage you to teach your students to do the same.

40

Name _____ Date _____

Music Exercise _____

Today's assessment focused on the three skills or concepts named below. The checked boxes show the skills or concepts demonstrated satisfactorily. Empty boxes show the skills or concepts needing more attention.

☐

☐

☐

Comments:

☐ Use my comments and keep practicing this exercise to continue to improve your performance. Be sure to talk to me if you have questions or need help. Replay this exercise:

_____

☐ Assignment complete.

Form 1.1: Early Skills

Name _____ Date _____

Music Exercise _____

The checked boxes show two elements of your performance that were particularly strong.

☐ Key signature   Comments:
☐ Pitches
☐ Intonation
☐ Rhythm
☐ Pulse
☐ Bowing style
☐ Technique
☐ Tone
☐ Phrasing
☐ Dynamics

The checked box shows one element for you to think about as you continue to practice.

☐ Key signature   Comments:
☐ Pitches
☐ Intonation
☐ Rhythms
☐ Pulse
☐ Bowing style
☐ Technique
☐ Tone
☐ Phrasing
☐ Dynamics

☐ Use my comments and keep practicing this exercise. Be sure to talk to me if you have questions or need help. Replay exercise:

_____

☐ Assignment complete.

Form 1.2: Developing Fundamentals

42

Name _____ Date _____

Music Exercise _____

1. What is one area that needs improvement in your playing?

☐ Notes   ☐ Technique

☐ Intonation   ☐ Tone

☐ Rhythm and pulse   ☐ Dynamics

☐ Bowing style   ☐ _____

2. Explain why you think this area needs improvement.

_____

_____

3. What did you do when you practiced to improve in this area?

_____

_____

_____

_____

Teacher's Comments:

Form 1.3: Individual Improvement Goal

Name _____ Date _____

Scale _____

Circled notes in the scale were played as a wrong note.

                                1

                        7   7

                    6   6

                5   5

              4   4

            3   ·   3

          2   2

        1   1

Comments:

☐ Use my comments and keep practicing this scale to play it accurately. Be
sure to talk to me if you have questions or need help. Replay this scale:

_____

☐ Scale satisfactory. Assignment complete.

Form 2.1: Early Scales

44

Name _____ Date _____

Scale _____

Improvement is needed in the areas circled:

Comments:

Clean Start

Correct Notes

Intonation

Even Tone

Steady Tempo

Expected Tempo

☐ Use my comments and keep practicing this scale. Be sure to talk to me if you have questions or need help. Replay this scale:

_____

☐ Scale proficient. Assignment complete.

Form 2.2: Scale Proficiency

Name _____ Date _____

Music Exercise _____

_____ or _____ played incorrectly are written in each
measure box:

①   ②   ③   ④

⑤   ⑥   ⑦   ⑧

Comments:

_____   _____   _____   Total

_____ + _____ + _____ = _____

  (8)   (1)   (1)   (10)

Form 3.1: Eight-Measure Exercise

Name _____

Exercise and Rhythm	Comments		Points* (8)
#_____	Count and Clap	(Date:)	
	Play	(Date:)	
#_____	Count and Clap	(Date:)	
	Play	(Date:)	
#_____	Count and Clap	(Date:)	
	Play	(Date:)	
#_____	Count and Clap	(Date:)	
	Play	(Date:)	

*Every exercise may be repeated on _____ to show mastery.

Form 3.2: Special Focus—Rhythm

Name _____

Special Focus_____

Exercise	Comments	Points* (8)
	(Date:)	
	(Date:)	
	(Date:)	
	(Date:)	

*Every exercise may be repeated on _____ to show mastery.

Form 3.3: Special Focus

Name _____ Date _____

Music Excerpt _____

Instrument _____

Element	3 points	2 points	1 point

Total Score _____

Comments:

☐ Use my comments and keep practicing this excerpt to play it accurately.
Be sure to talk to me if you have questions or need help.
Replay this excerpt:

_____

☐ Excerpt satisfactory. Assignment complete.

Form 4.1: Concert Repertoire